We Have an Altar

We Have an Altar

A Series of
Communion Meditations

CLARENCE TUCKER CRAIG

Professor of New Testament Language and Literature
Oberlin Graduate School of Theology

THE ABINGDON PRESS

NEW YORK   CINCINNATI   CHICAGO

CRAIG
WE HAVE AN ALTAR

Copyright, 1934, by
CLARENCE TUCKER CRAIG

Printed in the United States of America

Contents

Worship Through Communion

THE revival of an emphasis upon worship is a noteworthy characteristic of modern Protestantism. Its significance does not lie in a return to ritualism. True worship always has the passion for reality. If forms are acquiring a new meaning, it is from the realization that the narrow experience of a single individual cannot carry us as far into a knowledge of God as the experience of the race. It is likewise false to stigmatize this emphasis as a retreat from the ethical tasks of religion. True worship brings empowerment for their realization.

Not always, however, has a stress upon the Lord's Supper accompanied this revival of worship. The tendency persists in Protestantism for the eucharist to become "an optional appendage." There are some who find in it a meaningless superstition rather than a means of grace. If the primary place of the Lord's Supper is to be maintained in the modern church, three things are necessary.

First: It must be exalted as a primary experience of worship. It should not be an appendix to a service otherwise complete, but the climax of a unitary service. This is more and more being recognized in the building of special orders of service for the

celebration of communion. Therefore we would lay
the emphasis upon worship as an *immediate* experience and not simply a derivative and secondary
experience. The special danger arises from too ex-
clusive a stress upon the factor of commemoration in
connection with the Lord's Supper. It will never
be forgotten that events in an upper room nineteen
hundred years ago are bound by sacred association
with the communion service. But a primary experience of worship must be more than a memorial. It
must provide direct contact with the living God. It
cannot be said too often that the Lord's Supper is
not a funeral service, but the sacred meal at which
the living Christ is host. Around the symbolism of
food, a service of *worship* is built. As in all worship,
it is worship of God. It celebrates what he has done
for men. It evokes our sacrificial dedication. It
sets forth the gift of grace and the response of
obedience.

*Second: Continuous teaching must be provided to
set forth the meaning of the rite.* This is the justification for the Communion meditation. Not a few
ministers believe that they should conduct a strictly
ritualistic service, excluding all personal remarks. It
seems to me that this custom neglects the most perti-
nent opportunity to bring home some aspect of this
many-sided rite. It may be pointed out that in a

ritualistic church, such as the Anglican, the *only* service at which a sermon is properly in order is at holy communion. There are types of discourse which are quite out of place, but meditations upon many of the mysteries of faith are nowhere as fitting as at this hour. The teaching ministry of the church must not neglect her own sacraments. Symbols are not meaningful unless accompanied by expositions of their significance. In the past the central position of the eucharist was assured by its relation to the conception of redemption which men held. Some of the older conceptions of redemption are no longer vital to our worshipers. Our people do not quickly relate the Lord's Supper to the realities of a redemptive process within them. If the centrality of the service is to be maintained, there is a task laid upon the teaching ministry of the church.

Third: We need to recapture the manifold meanings associated with this one rite in the first century. It was a thanksgiving for the various blessings of God. It was a commemoration of those blessings, especially of the death of Christ for men. It was for some of them a sacrifice; that is, the bread and wine were offered unto God as an expression of the offering of themselves. It was a rite of communion with Christ, and through him with God; at the same time it was a service of fellowship in his one body—the church. It represented the ratification of a new divine ordinance bringing the forgiveness of sins, and again it was an anticipation of the return of their risen Lord. Others no longer thought of his return; they found the mystical presence of their Saviour in this communion meal. It was to them the mystery of feeding upon the bread of heaven.

Such a bare catalogue does not begin to exhaust the wealth of associations with which the early Christians surrounded the rite. It is less important that we try to revive ideas no longer natural for us than that we follow their example and bring out new meanings which we may discover in the symbolism surrounding food in our approach to God. Our aim cannot be to recover some primitive model, but to follow the leading of the Spirit in the development of a rite for the twentieth century. It is of the very genius of religion that acts persist; their meanings change. But the first step in preparing to interpret the Lord's Supper to the twentieth century is to enter fully into the heritage which we possess from the first.

The meditations included in this little volume have all grown out of a pastoral ministry to individual congregations. Each one has had a history, so that I can no longer trace all of the indebtedness which readers are sure to find. Their publication arises from a need discovered in teaching a course on "The Communion" in the theological seminary. Of expositions of doctrine there are many. Scholarly exegetical studies are fewer in English, but not entirely lacking. Of devotional treatments in the spirit and language of the modern age, I have been able to call the attention of students to only a few. This little volume is sent forth with the hope that it may stimulate others to share their meditations upon the mystery of Communion.

A Purpose for Existence

IN a certain factory you could find until recently during every working day a woman sitting before a moving belt. As thousands of eggs passed by, it was her duty to tap each one lightly on the tip in order to crack the shell. For thirty years during ten hours each day she performed this task. Underneath that picture let us insert as a trial title: "To this end have I been born, and to this end am I come into the world."

If that sounds a little ridiculous, just recite to yourself the day of a typical friend. If you have the temerity, try to attach these words to your own daily round. Then, what a contrast there is when we turn to the life of Jesus! He impresses us with an overwhelming sense of mission. "I am come not to destroy the law, but to fulfill." "I am come not to call the righteous, but sinners." "The Son of man is come to seek and to save them that are lost." "I am come that they might have life, and that they might have it abundantly." It was not that he neglected the secondary ends of life. "The Son of man came eating and drinking," and the religious zealots of his time misunderstood this normal social intercourse. But he subordinated all minor objectives to a great aim so that he could say before Pilate's judgment bar, "To this end have I been born, and to this end am I come into the world, that I should bear witness unto the truth." Jesus was here for a purpose, and it gave meaning to every hour of his life.

Man is a seeker of ends. Life means activity, and action is related to a purpose. Most of our aims are secondary, valuable and necessary, but finding their ultimate justification only in something beyond them. For all of us, some drudgery is inescapable, some amusement necessary, but these provide no primary goal for life. It cannot be said with due perspective of these, "For this cause came I into the world." Gamaliel Bradford said of Edward Fitzgerald, "Like many people who have no main object in life, he was often busy from morning till night." Those words could be written in the life story of multitudes. They frazzle out at the ends in their pursuit of many secondary goals. They are so busy about many things that they have no time for one thing that is needful.

Man at his best has demanded that there be some purpose at the heart of the universe itself. He may not be able to find it; he certainly is not able to prove it. The apparently accidental and haphazard thrust themselves continually before us, but man clings to the faith that there is a divinity that shapes our ends and the ends of all creation. The faith arises from our discovery of the futility of any existence without a purpose. If the universe be a ship adrift with no port in view, if it be simply a revolving wheel, then all striving is a hideous farce and all planning but the chase of will-o'-the wisps. Christianity has spoken of a plan of salvation. We may discard some of its theological presuppositions, but it expresses a Christian faith in a goal "to which the whole creation moves."

Whether this demand upon the universe be true or false, at least there can be no doubt of the demand which the universe makes upon us. "No life can realize a high degree of development without the strict subordination of many cravings which conflict with a worth-while central aim." "Life should be more than a long, dismal conjugation of the word, 'to eat.'" We are more than log-wood drifting down a stream. We must chart a course, fix a goal, set our compass, and buffet every contrary wind. At this time when business firms are opening new ledgers and taking inventory of their assets, we would do well to take stock of ourselves. What are we here for? For what cause have we come into the world?

There is not one goal in life, but many. There is not one value, but many things that are truly worth while. Happiness and beauty, love and truth all belong in the pattern of the rich life. No two paths can be the same, nor can these values be combined in the same proportion. Wherever we have found the pearl, we must suffer and sacrifice that which is good to attain it. How many of us there are who cannot make up our minds and wobble between conflicting aims and never attain! How many of us there are who never find ourselves! We may find work that provides a competence, but life for us has never acquired a sense of mission nor a purpose that gives reason to existence.

Since we are met together as members and friends of this church, may we ask if it has a purpose for existence. As every other organization, it has to expend so much energy simply in keeping its wheels turning round that we often forget to ask what it is all about. We hold meetings, raise budgets, exhort to loyalty to the institution without inquiring whether all this endeavor simply perpetuates futility. Since the fires of hell have burned low, a redemptive purpose no longer motivates many in their devotion to the church. But an institution without a clear-cut sense of mission has lost its excuse for being.

The church is not here primarily to provide a

substitute for other concrete interests of life; it is not to compete with the lodge, nor the movie, nor the athletic club, but to cultivate that which will give meaning to it all. It is to help men enter into a living appreciation of the crowning arch over all of life; to cultivate in a world obsessed with the production of the useful the worship of the holy; to promote reverence for all life and personality, for it is made in the image of the Divine; to further the joyful acceptance of the law of love, for God is love.

New Year's Eve found the restaurants filled with diners eating the last supper of the old year and drinking a toast amid shouts and revelry to the new-born year. We are reminded of two last suppers which are recounted in the Book of books. At one, Belshazzar, the king of Babylonia, gave a feast for a thousand of his lords. The wine flowed freely, and the king's wives and concubines joined in the company. They praised the gods of gold and of silver, of brass, of iron, of wood, and of stone. Then the king was startled by a man's hand writing on the wall words that none of his wise men could interpret. Into the midst of that scene of purposeless revelry came the warning of the doom which was sealed for a man who had come into the world for no other purpose than to eat and drink and be merry and exercise the power that fortune had bestowed upon him. The cup that they passed was a sacrament of doom.

Since the other supper has become a sacred mystery, we tend to forget the pregnant simplicity of the scene. On the night in which he was betrayed Jesus sat at supper in the upper room with a faithful little band of disciples who had followed him to Jerusalem. As the humble meal drew to a close, he took bread, and brake it, and giving it to his disciples, said, "This is my body, which is for you." And as he distributed a cup, it is reported that he repeated similar words, "This is my blood which is poured out for many." He went out from that room to meet his captors; he went out to testify before Pilate's judgment seat, "To this end am I come into the world." His last supper was a sacrament of dedication.

What cup shall we drink as we toast the New Year? Do we welcome three hundred and sixty-five aimless days, or does one controlling purpose bend every fugitive energy to the end for which we live? Shall we drink a sacrament of doom, or a sacrament of dedication as we pledge our lives, "For this cause came I into the world"?

TABLE DISMISSALS

1. We have come into the world to pursue truth and shun falsehood; to follow it wherever it may

lead; throughout that quest, may the peace of God go with you.

2. We have come to love righteousness and not merely to accept correctness. As you leave the table of Him whose meat was to do the Father's will, may his peace go with you.

3. We have come to create beauty and to redeem the waste places of the earth. As you leave the table of Him who was altogether lovely, may his peace go with you.

4. We have come to subdue the earth and to conquer it for mankind. As you leave the table of Him whom the wind and the waves obeyed, may his peace go with you.

5. We have come into the world to have fellowship with man. As you leave the table of Him who was called Son of man, may peace with all his brethren go with you.

6. We have come in order to have fellowship with God. As you leave the table of Him who opened a new and living way into his presence, may the divine peace go with you.

7. We have come in order to find life that is abundant, full, and free. As you leave the table of Him in whom was the Life that was the light of men, may the peace of God go with you.

He Who Is Faithful

IN the municipal Art Gallery at Glasgow hangs an impressive picture of the destruction of Pompeii. There is only one color tone, a glowing red as of a blast furnace. Hot masses of lava are falling through the roof of the house; partitions are giving way; in the distance, retreating figures of men and women run hither and thither vainly seeking to escape from the rain of fire. One form stands erect and motionless in the foreground, still protecting the entrance to the luxurious home. It is the Roman guard, tightly clasping his spear, "faithful unto death."

That is not our common experience with men. The Wisdom writer described it vividly when he coined the aphorism, "Most men will proclaim everyone his own kindness, but a faithful man, who can find? . . . Confidence in an unfaithful man in time of trouble is *like* a broken tooth, and a foot out of joint." It is all too true. Man is fitful and unstable. Every leader knows the fickleness of the popular mind. It is proverbial to speak of the "faithful few."

The supreme question for religion is whether God is as variable as man, or whether he is faithful. Is God dependable? Is he, as James wrote, "the Father of lights, in whom is no shadow of turning"? Does his faithfulness endure unto all generations?

The importance of this question becomes even more apparent when we see how large a place in religion has been occupied with attempts to persuade God to change his mind. The prayers of primitive men reveal the supposition that their gods were creatures such as they, to be moved by effective persuasion. Such primitive religion is to be found among many so-called Christians who likewise look upon God—whenever they do think of him—as a choreboy to be wheedled and coaxed. But the psalmist said, "He is the rock of my salvation." When we are tossing in a boat, we do not expect to pull the rock to us; we want a firm anchorage to which we may draw ourselves. If the "Rock of Ages" is a fitting symbol of the Eternal, it would show that the purposes of the Lord are not to be commanded but to be understood. He is fixed and faithful.

It is science which has done more than anything else to enforce upon the modern mind that we must think of God as faithful. Not that science can speak on such ultimate questions as the existence of God, but its postulates do have weight as to *how* we may think of him. Science believes that this is a world of dependable law where experiment can lead to the discovery of truth. We do not have angry spirits to placate, but dependable processes to understand. The natives of Formosa go head-hunting in the spring, for they believe that a human skull in the field will promote fertility of the soil. We know that productivity depends upon nitrates and fertile seeds, upon moisture and sunshine, and no incantations can avail where these are absent. It is a tremendous relief to learn that bacteria and diseased imaginations, not evil spirits, bring visitations upon mankind. Man is not helpless because we live in a law-abiding universe, for there is some hope of control in a world where effect follows cause.

What is the meaning of this for religion? It certainly means that prayer should not descend to the level of a magic which would compel the gods to do our will. It means that faithfulness is the mark of any worthy God. The Bible was written before the dawn of science; we will not expect it to answer questions of scientific fact. But significantly the faithfulness of God is a theme which runs from Genesis to the Revelation of John. "Covenant" and "promise" are two words that run throughout the Old Testament. Originally they were taken as a very materialistic pledge to the Jewish people. They came to mean all the benefits which might flow from a spiritual God.

In the New Testament the key word seems to be "faith"; we are accustomed to summarize Protestant doctrine as salvation by faith in contrast to salvation by human works. But in popular statement faith often seems to be only a little more spiritual work of merit than making pilgrimages, burning candles, and giving alms. That misses entirely the profound insight of Paul. He looked upon faith as itself a gift of God. Men were not saved by their own mental attitudes, but by the faithfulness of God. It is striking that the same Greek word may be translated "faith," or "faithfulness." It is the faithfulness of God's own character, his steadfast purpose of good will in which we can implicitly trust. That understanding helps us to see what Paul means when he wrote, "And whom he foreordained, them he also called; and whom he called, them he also justified: and whom he justified, them he also glorified." We should forget all such technical terms of theology, and hear the triumphant word that God's long purpose for humanity will be realized, for he is faithful.

But is it true? Can we still believe it? There is little to be gained for Paul to write it or for the minister to proclaim it if I cannot verify it in my own experience. It is the loyal heart which discovers to the full the faithfulness that is manifested toward us. In 2 Timothy we read those well-known words, "I have fought a good fight; I have finished my course; I have kept the faith." As sometimes interpreted, "keeping the faith" is maintaining the purity of catholic doctrine. But we know that in the genuine letters of Paul "faith" is not a body of doctrine to be preserved. We see the genuine Paul when we learn that the words were the usual phrase for "holding true." Paul is saying, "I have fought a good fight. . . . I have kept faith." It is through his own loyalty that Paul has discovered the faithfulness of God. It is through our increasing steadfastness that we learn that God is the one upon whom we may always depend.

We shall spend no time this morning brooding over the occasions when we have broken our resolutions, when we have proved disloyal to the best we knew, unfaithful to those who trusted us. We would approach to-morrow with higher resolve. From ancient times men have pledged their faithfulness by drinking together. The communion cup has been interpreted to us as an emblem of the self-giving of Christ on the cross. The eternal meaning of Calvary is God's pledge of faithfulness toward man, his utmost endeavor to lift man from his degradation. As we drink of this cup may it be for us the pledge of our faithfulness. May our prayer be that the body that feeds upon the broken bread and the wine poured out for us, and the soul that feeds upon the spiritual bread of heaven, may be as steadfast as was the Lord of Life who gave himself for us.

To us the injunction is ever fresh, "That good thing which was committed unto thee, guard through the Holy Spirit." "Be thou faithful unto the end." And we answer back in words of assurance, "For I know whom I have believed, and am persuaded that he is able to keep that which I have committed unto him against that day." For God is faithful.

TABLE DISMISSALS

1. If we confess our sins, He is faithful and righteous to forgive us our sins, and to cleanse us from all unrighteousness. In the strength of that promise, may you go in peace.

2. Consider the Apostle and High Priest of our confession, even Jesus; who was faithful to Him that appointed him as also was Moses in all his house. With the same steadfastness, may you go in peace.

3. God is faithful, who will not suffer you to be tempted above that ye are able; but will with the temptation make also the way of escape. In this confidence, may you go in peace.

4. May it be said of you, "Well done, good and

[25]

faithful servant; thou hast been faithful over a few things; enter thou into the joy of thy Lord."

5. Let us hold fast the confession of our hope that it waver not; for He is faithful that promised. In that assurance, may you go in peace.

6. Jesus said, "He that is faithful in a very little is faithful also in much. If therefore ye have not been faithful in the unrighteous mammon, who will commit to your trust the true riches?" May you go from this table to that trust and may you go in peace.

7. Such confidence have we through Christ to Godward; not that we are sufficient of ourselves, but our sufficiency is from God. Trusting in his faithfulness, may you go in peace.

The Broken Body

THERE is always pathos in a broken body. You have seen bodies broken with toil, backs bent, chest stooped, fingers gnarled and twisted. You have seen bodies, strong bodies, broken by grief. You have seen bodies broken by disease, wasted by tuberculosis, blinded by cataracts, burned with fever. The psalmist said that "the sacrifices of God are a broken spirit," but a broken body may represent many kinds of sacrifices.

The first time I went down Friedrichstrasse in Berlin at the close of the Great War, the shell-shocked and maimed lay asking alms. They seemed to say to each passer-by in mute testimony, "This is my body, which is broken for you." But behind every front were two kinds of hospitals. There were those treating soldiers who had been wounded in battle. There were also those treating patients whose own vice had incapacitated them for service. We need think only of the ravages of alcohol and drugs to call to mind the long list of those who are wounded for their own transgressions, and bruised

[27]

for their own iniquities, and whose stripes are the prison stripes by which no one is healed. They come to the end of their days to say to the Creator of all life, "This is my body, which is broken for my own indulgence and sin."

There can be no doubt that Jesus' body was broken. He healed men's diseases, but he never spared himself. The gospel writer emphasized the fulfillment of the prophecy, "Not one of his bones is broken." That was only because he had died long before the usual time. It is difficult for us to picture the physical and mental strain under which Jesus spent his last days. I cannot quite put away the guess that he chose to ride on an animal into Jerusalem after the long climb from Jericho because of the pressure of fatigue. If that be fanciful, we at least know that the Man who fought a losing fight with the ruling hierarchy, whose head had not touched a pillow the previous night, and whose body had been scourged with cruel thongs, fell under the load of the cross and another had to be pressed into service. It was a body already broken that was nailed to the tree.

> "O sacred Head, now wounded,
>   With grief and shame weighed down,
> Now scornfully surrounded
>   With thorns, thine only crown."

In his case, there can be no doubt for whom that body was broken. It was not for himself that he braved his foes, but for the cause to which he had given his life. We are the inheritors of that cause; but we still commit the same sins that nailed him to the cross. Hence it is not exaggeration when the hymn writer sings,

"We may not know, we cannot tell
What pains he had to bear;
But we believe it was for us
He hung and suffered there."

The Romans placed an inscription over the cross in Latin, Greek, and Hebrew, "Jesus of Nazareth, the King of the Jews." History has spelled out another sentence: "This is my body, which is broken for you."

One of the most striking expressions of Paul was to speak of the church as the "body of Christ." A body is a visible instrument through which the spirit finds expression. A tomb could not contain the body of Christ; it found resurrection in the Christian Church which carried on the ministry of the ascended Lord. As the spirit of the Christ who walked in Galilee and Jerusalem was manifest unto men through a body, so down through the ages it must be mediated unto men through some other instrument. May we lift our vision this morning from petty proceedings and quarreling groups and crumbling buildings to that thought of the church as the continuing body of Christ.

It is unfortunately a broken body. We see the hand saying to the eye or the ear, that it has no need of them, or that they really are no part of the body. It is a body broken by theological controversies, mutual jealousies, and racial and social discrimination. The one hundred and twenty-six groups in America calling themselves Christian, present not a body but a mosaic. We hope and pray that reunion may come. It is not that we may create an institution of power that will be tempted to depart still further from the spirit of Christ. It is that his body may continually be broken for men.

I fear that the man on the street rarely thinks of the church as a body broken for him. He thinks of the church as an institution supremely concerned with its own perpetuation. Why is it that a Hindu student should have gotten the impression while in America that if India were to have any religion at all, it would be best for it to be Christian, for "it costs so little"? It could not be if the voice of every church were resonant and clear in acts as well as words, "This is his body, which is broken for you."

There is still a third sense in which we would consider the broken body. We have already seen that the essence of a body is not found in chemical substance or physical structure. A body is the effective instrument through which the spirit reaches men. Let us not be led aside by thoughts of the miraculous transformation of particles of wheat. But as Christ needed a body in which to perform his own ministry, as Christ needs to-day the body of the church through which to minister unto men, so likewise for the sake of communion with him we may truly say of the broken bread, "This is my body, which is broken for you."

If you read the Revised Version, you will not find the word "broken." It is not in the earliest texts. Whoever added it knew that the breaking of bread introduced the meal. It was the symbolic action which our Lord had performed. It was more than a preparation of the loaf for distribution. It was a parable of the complete giving of himself to the disciples. As this bread was broken and given to them, so would his body be broken for them.

Some are glad that it is a broken body with which we commune. They desire to select and choose only a part of what is offered. They would partake of the comfort of Christ, but not his challenge. They would have his peace, but not his conflict on behalf of right. They would have his crown, but not his cross. The body of Christ is not broken that we may select the delectable portions; it is broken in order that the whole Christ may be available for all men. It is broken in order to symbolize the consecrated spirit which was his and should be ours. With yearning hearts we pray,

"Bread of thy Body, give me for my fighting,
Give me to drink thy sacred blood for wine,
While there are wrongs that need me for the righting,
While there is warfare splendid and divine."

There answers back to our souls, "This is my body, which is broken for you."

TABLE DISMISSALS

1. God forbid that I should glory, save in the cross of our Lord Jesus Christ, though which the world hath been crucified unto me and I unto the world.

2. "See, from his head, his hands, his feet,
Sorrow and love flow mingled down!
Did e'er such love and sorrow meet,
Or thorns compose so rich a crown?"

3. Christ also suffered for sins once, the righteous for the unrighteous, that he might bring us to God.

4. "In the cross of Christ I glory,
      Towering o'er the wrecks of time;
   All the light of sacred story
      Gathers round its head sublime."

5. The word of the cross is to them that are perishing foolishness, but to us who are being saved it is the power of God and the wisdom of God.

6. "Let the water and the blood,
      From thy wounded side which flowed,
   Be of sin the double cure,
      Save from wrath and make me pure."

7. For God so loved the world, that he gave his only begotten Son, that whosoever believeth on him should not perish, but have eternal life.

The Cup

THERE is a curious lack of parallelism which is maintained throughout all of the accounts of the Last Supper. In one case Jesus speaks of the food; in the other, of the vessel. He took bread and said, "This is my body." He took the cup and said, "This is my blood." It is not the bread and wine, nor the plate and the cup, but, rather, the bread and the cup. In fact, in the early church the cup was often filled with water instead of wine.

Too much significance should not be ascribed to this distinction, for there may be sufficient explanation in the customs of table fellowship. The bread was not cut and lying on a plate, but was a single, unleavened loaf that was broken in the hand. No one can pass wine except in some kind of cup. And yet I find a certain symbolic significance in the phrase, "the cup." It is used over and over again in the Bible to mean more than a mere container of liquids. At the Jewish Passover four separate cups were drunk, each with its own particular meaning. In preparation for the receiving of Christ's testamental cup, may we meditate on four different cups which we may drink.

The first of these is the *cup of divine wrath.* The phrase appears over and over again in the Old-Testament prophets. For the sins of Israel, Jehovah would pour out the cup of his wrath upon them. In only one book of the New Testament does it appear, in the book of Revelation, which for all of its note of hope seems to us at many places to fall short of a true Christian spirit. Yet we can appreciate why the seer felt that if anyone had pledged allegiance to the Lord Jesus Christ, when he bowed to the imperial worship of Cæsar he would drink of "the wine of the wrath of God which is prepared unmixed in the cup of his anger."

I have no intention of preaching that message this morning, but we are apt to forget that Christ's gospel is one of moral earnestness. How can you offer to men a cup of salvation if they continue to remain in their sins? Jesus spoke in no mild terms of those who cleansed the outside of the cup when within they were full of extortion and excess. Paul warned the Corinthians that they might drink judgment unto themselves. If we take the communion cup in smiling complacency or downright hypocrisy, how can it be for us other than the cup of divine wrath?

Jesus reveals a God who is in earnest about moral character. He calls for a candid sincerity and simplicity of life, a humble and repentant spirit.

Though we know that we fall short of his ideal, we should not stay away from the Lord's table in superstitious fear. This is not an altar for those who imagine that they are perfect, but for those who sincerely repent of their sins, and desire to lead a new and better life.

The second cup of which we may drink is the *cup of sorrow*. Jesus went out from the upper room into the garden of Gethsemane. There, in apprehension of his tragic end, he poured out his soul unto God. "Abba, Father, all things are possible unto thee; remove this cup from me: howbeit, not what I will, but what thou wilt." You remember likewise the time when two of the disciples came to him with the plea that they might sit one on his right hand and the other on his left. Jesus replied, "Are ye able to drink the cup that I drink?" It was the cup of suffering and sorrow.

It is instructive that Jesus accepted the cup of sorrow from God's hand. I do not believe that Jesus wanted to drink that cup any more than we crave suffering and trial. The answer to his prayer came not in the removal of the cup but in the strength to drink it. What seemed at the moment to be a terrible evil could work out for good.

When the cup of sorrow is passed to us, it is easy to confuse it with the cup of divine wrath. Feeling that the suffering is undeserved, we rebel at the apparent injustice. We have no satisfactory explanation of the distribution of sorrow, but this we know, that it is not a demonstration of God's anger. The world's great sufferers have included the world's greatest saints.

The third cup is the *cup of fellowship*. We drink together as a symbol of fellowship. Though "wine is a mocker, strong drink is raging," nevertheless, we should not forget that some of the oldest social customs surround the flowing bowl. We have rightly abolished the common drinking cup in the interest of sanitation, but we must maintain the common cup of fellowship at all costs.

As the disciples of Jesus drank together, their communion was more closely knit. As they drank in similar fashion after his death, they maintained fellowship with him. Paul could speak of the cup as a "communion of the blood of Christ." It brought his followers into blood fellowship with him; thus they became one body in him.

Paul's words come in the midst of a discussion which, literally interpreted, has no relevance for us. Some of his converts had apparently continued to eat and drink at pagan idol feasts. Paul warns them, "You cannot drink both the cup of demons and the cup of Christ." We have our modern equivalents of the cup of demons, that divide men from one another and from Christ. We must choose that with which we will hold communion. Christ extends to us this morning the cup of his fellowship. We cannot drink at the same time of the demons of jealousy and prejudice, envy and malice, for his cup pledges a bond of love.

One final thought: Paul designates this cup as the *"cup of blessing* which we bless." It is true that in our ritual we pronounce words of blessing over the cup, but it is God alone who can make of it a true cup of blessing. It is his blessing we seek; his mercy we would find.

At the Jewish Passover one of the cups was a cup of blessing. The ancient pastoral festival was interpreted as a remembrance of God's merciful deliverance of the children of Israel from their slavery in Egypt. There had followed a covenant sealed in blood between Jehovah and his people. At the Christian supper they repeated these words, "This cup is the new covenant in my blood." Herein lay the blessing, the new testament of God's gracious will for mankind.

Jesus passes a cup of blessing. It is not for one race but for all men. It commemorates not the giving of a law but the giving of a life. The giving of that life is a symbol of the gracious mercy of God toward all who repent. The cup is the cup of his blessing freely given to you.

TABLE DISMISSALS

1. "I will take the cup of salvation and call upon the name of the Lord." You have received his cup; you have heard his word of assurance; may you go in peace.

2. If you have been drinking of the cup of sorrow, may the angels of God's comfort come and minister to you and send you from the table of the Lord in peace.

3. Paul said, "Ye cannot drink the cup of the Lord, and the cup of demons." May the demons of fear and worry, of hatred and greed, be driven out, that we may drink the cup of the Lord in peace.

4. Jesus said, "Ye make clean the outside of the cup, but within are full of extortion and uncleanness." With hearts that are purified we come to drink his cup, and within ourselves find peace.

5. "My cup runneth over;" these words of the psalmist express our joy as we partake of the cup of blessing. Go in peace.

6. When Jesus took the cup, he gave thanks. If it is God's cup, whatever it contains, we may drink it with thanksgiving. As you give thanks, may you go in peace.

7. The search for the Holy Grail is one of the world's most beautiful legends. As we leave this table may it be in remembrance that the true Grail is not a golden chalice, but a cup shared with needy humanity. With that conviction, may you go in peace.

The Remission of Sins

THE communion rituals of most churches embody the words in the Gospel of Matthew, "This is my blood of the covenant, which is poured out for many unto remission of sins." From very early time this has been one of the thoughts associated with communion. I want you to think with me upon them this morning, for they suggest one of the permanent perils to spiritual religion—the idea that sacrifices afford access to God.

Sacrifices for sin are as ancient as religion. In Israel expiation for sins was sought through burnt-offerings and the sacrifice of bulls and sheep and goats. It was thought that an offended Deity must be satisfied through gifts and oblations. Against this whole system, the great prophets hurled the fury of their condemnation. The word of Jehovah came to them, "I will have mercy and not sacrifice. . . . I delight not in the blood of bulls." What God desires is justice, love, and righteousness, for only these can bring men into right relation with him.

It is never easy for religion to be maintained on a high spiritual plane. When Jesus came to the Temple at Jerusalem, he found an elaborate sacrificial worship. Of course the old prophetic insistence upon repentance had not been entirely superseded, but it was thought that the sacrifices had to be maintained if men were to be sure of God's favor. Jesus proclaimed unconditionally unto men that if they repented of their sin, God was ready and anxious to forgive. We read in the Gospels how he gave the word of assurance. We see in such stories as the parable of the prodigal son how he conceived of the readiness of God to pardon. It waited upon no sacrifice; it was consummated by no sacrament; he brought the good news of a forgiving God.

But a world that was accustomed to sacrifice could not refrain from importing sacrificial ideas into the Christian gospel. Already in the New Testament we find the death of Christ interpreted as the one and sufficient sacrifice for sin. In the later church the Lord's Supper came to be looked upon as a sacrifice, not simply the offering unto God of the bread and wine, but such a re-presentation of the death of Christ as would assure unto participants its atoning benefits. Deeply embedded as this language is in the hymnology and ritual of the church, nevertheless men are seeing that they cannot believe with

[42]

the prophets and Jesus and at the same time believe
that forgiveness is brought by a sacrifice, even by
the self-offering of Jesus.

Remission is not a familiar word in common
speech. Almost our only connection is with words at
the bottom of a statement—"Please remit." They
indicate that something stands between us and
another party; there is an obligation that is unmet.
So sins have been interpreted as a debt to God and
it has sometimes been said that Jesus paid the debt.
If one thing is clear from the story Jesus told about
two debtors, it is that the gospel can never be stated
in the language of business. Debts of money may
be paid by a substitute, but debts of love and gratitude can be paid only by those contracting.

The remission of sin is not like unto a financial
transaction where we may draw on the credit of the
merits of Christ. It is the restoration of fellowship
between man and God. It is the removal of that
which separates; it could not be removed by any one
event. As Studdert Kennedy, that rugged preacher
of the cross, once said, "The cross didn't save the
world from sin. Sin and sorrow still continue. . . .
Men still torture men and women, children still go
hungry, there is still rape and murder, lust and war.
Our streets are full of it; our papers ring with it;
the world remains unsaved." But the cross remains

[43]

the supreme appeal of the divine heart for man to repent of his sins.

The Gospels make it plain that divine forgiveness waits upon one thing. It did not wait for Calvary; it does not wait for our reception of the symbols of the sufferings and passion of Jesus. It waits for the forgiving spirit in the hearts of men. We were taught to pray, "Forgive us our trespasses, as we forgive those that trespass against us." "For if ye forgive men their trespasses, your heavenly Father will also forgive you. But if ye forgive not men their trespasses, neither will your Father forgive your trespasses."

In the Apostles' Creed there is the great affirmation—"I believe in the forgiveness of sins." We may have thought of that only as a comfort that my own sins will be forgiven. There is no more challenging clause in the entire creed. In the light of the teaching of Jesus it can only mean that I believe in forgiving wrongs against me, for that is the only possible ground of restoration to fellowship with God. Our own repentance is genuine only when we show a forgiving attitude toward others.

Did Jesus do nothing for the forgiveness of sins? To say that would be to miss the most glorious word in the gospel. He did forgive the publican and sinner, the outcast and erring. The word of forgiveness became flesh in him and dwelt among men, and seeing him, men could believe that God was gracious. It was when Jean Valjean saw the word of forgiveness become flesh in the person of the Bishop of D. that hope and faith and goodness were reborn in him. It is only as the word of forgiveness becomes flesh in us that the good news of God will be believed to-day.

Are we to say, then, that the Lord's Supper has no relation to the forgiveness of sins? By no means; for it insists that communion with God is only possible for the repentant heart. We are invited to this table in one spirit and in one only, when we are "in love and charity with our neighbors and desire to lead a new life." The brotherhood of this sacred meal dare not be severed by an unforgiving spirit. There is no sacrifice that can avail except the sacrifice of our own contrite heart. This is a sacrament for the remission of sins because we must approach it in the forgiving spirit. Kneeling here there is no place for rancor or malice, no possibility of hatred or anger. Kneeling here there is full assurance of the forgiveness of sins, for it is the table of Him who in life and in death revealed the gracious mercy of God. We come unto One who "forgiveth all thine iniquities." We come at the invitation of Him who said, "Son, thy sins are forgiven thee." We come not with any merits of our own, but with contrite humility, gratefully to receive the remission of sins.

Table Dismissals

1. God was in Christ reconciling the world unto himself, not reckoning unto them their trespasses, and having committed unto us the word of reconciliation. Unto that ministry, go in peace.

2. On his knees as the stones of his slayers fell about him, Stephen cried out, "Lord, lay not this sin to their charge." In such a spirit may you go, and the consciousness of God's forgiveness bring you peace.

3. God hath "delivered us out of the power of darkness, and translated us into the kingdom of the Son of his love; in whom we have our redemption, the forgiveness of our sins." In that confidence, go in peace.

4. Jesus said, "If therefore thou art offering thy gift at the altar, and there rememberest that thy brother hath ought against thee, leave there thy gift before the altar, and go thy way, first be reconciled to thy brother, and then come and offer thy gift." With ungrudging heart, go in peace.

5. "If we confess our sins, he is faithful and righteous to forgive us our sins, and to cleanse us

from all unrighteousness." Go in peace and may peace abide with you.

6. "Be ye kind one to another, tender-hearted, forgiving each other, even as God also in Christ forgave you." To such a life may you go and the peace of God abide with you.

7. Jesus said, "Her sins, which are many, are forgiven; for she loved much: but to whom little is forgiven, the same loveth little." To great love may you go, and God's forgiveness and peace go with you.

𝕳𝖚𝖓𝖌𝖊𝖗

IN Knut Hamsun's masterpiece, *Hunger*, we read the struggle of a young writer with direst poverty. For days at a time the hero has not a morsel of food. Gruesome is the description of his attempt to eat raw meat off a bone, which he has gotten ostensibly for his dog. His empty, yet revolting, stomach casts off each bit. Hunger "gnawed unmercifully in my breast; carrying on a silent mysterious work in there. It was as if a score of diminutive gnome-like insects set their heads on one side and gnawed for a little, then laid their heads on the other side and gnawed a little more, then lay quite still for a moment's space, and then began afresh, boring noiselessly in, and without any haste, and left empty space everywhere after them as they went on."

Most remarkable of all was how the lust for food in the face of imminent starvation never drowned out the deeper hungers. Unstilled went on his unappeased hunger for human fellowship. Much deeper was his hunger for self-respect; when a breakfast was to be had at the police station for the asking and he had not had a meal for three days, he walked proudly out. Undiminished was his hunger for righteousness; direst want could not tempt him to dishonesty. Deepest of all was his longing for mental achievement as he penned the imaginings of his fevered brain.

Most of us have never known real physical hunger. We may read of famine conditions in China, or India, or Russia, but fortunately we know nothing of what it is for masses of people to be hungry. It is unfortunately true that business depression has brought bread-lines to our cities. During the war thousands of German and Austrian children suffered from malnutrition, and we shall have our human cost to pay in bodies permanently weakened from an insufficiency of the right kinds of food.

Malnutrition is, however, to be found not only among those who cannot buy enough food. It is surprising when school statistics show underweight and malnutrition in the children from wealthier homes. There are plenty of adults who likewise suffer, who eat not what will build a strong body, but the sweets that they fancy. Yet the number of people who count their calories, make certain of their vitamins, and watch their proteins and fats is fortunately on the increase. The importance of a sound diet is being recognized.

But certainly not all of us give enough attention

to a balanced diet for the whole man. Pork and poker, beef and bridge, mutton and movies are not sufficient to grow a healthy soul. Beer and pretzels do not feed the inner man. Arctic explorers have sometimes suffered from scurvy because they had no equivalent for fresh vegetables. There is likewise a spiritual scurvy which comes when some of the higher faculties receive no nourishment. It has often been noted that so eminent a man as Charles Darwin experienced the atrophy of musical appreciation and love of poetry in his intense devotion to biological research. It may seem necessary for some specialists so to concentrate upon their one purpose that noble faculties become starved. But the painful tragedy is that so many souls shrivel simply because they are not fed.

Sometimes we feel sorry for the hungry. As a matter of fact, loss of appetite is far worse. No teacher feels sorry for the boy or girl who is hungry for knowledge. A voracious longing to understand the experience of the race will insure a full life. It is those who are not hungry, who are content to live on starvation mental fare, who present the problem. No minister is sorry for the man or woman who is hungry for the living God. Religion arises out of a hunger for a larger life. "Man shall not live by bread alone, but by every word that proceedeth out of the mouth of God." Hence Jesus proclaimed, "Blessed are they that hunger and thirst after righteousness." Hunger is the condition of true blessedness. Only the hungry can be filled.

The gospel has sometimes been presented as medicine for sick souls; a much better figure is that of food for starved lives. It is that which John develops in his sixth chapter. The Israelites of old had been fed, according to tradition, by manna from heaven. The true, imperishable food was the bread of life which Jesus offered unto men. A figure of speech is always perilous. Like a pane of glass, it is something to look through, not to look at. To the Ephesian Christians who first read this gospel, it simply meant that Jesus met as fundamental a need in their lives as bread was for the sustenance of their bodies. The need for vision, for faith, for a moral ideal, for a foundation of hope, for an inspiration of love are all met in him. He is like unto a staff of life upon whom we may lean for spiritual sustenance. The chaff is driven away by the wind, but he is like wheat that nourisheth unto life.

It is in this chapter that John brings his eucharistic teaching. In strongly realistic words he insists that it is at the Lord's table that worshipers are to feed on this, the true bread of life. To eat the flesh and drink the blood is a symbol of the fullest appropriation to ourselves of the Lord of life. We trust in no magical transformation of these elements. The calories in the Lord's Supper will not appease the physical hunger of any man, nor will a few crumbs and a tiny sip in themselves satisfy a soul. We are invited in this ancient symbol to "feed on him in our hearts by faith with thanksgiving." We believe that the God of our Lord Jesus Christ is really present; but whether we rise from this table filled or empty depends upon the inner receptiveness with which we come.

It is a very old custom of the church that communicants should come to the table of the Lord before they have partaken of other food. We do not require physical fasting before communion. It is nevertheless true, that the table of the Lord is for the hungry. It is for those who hunger and thirst after a better life. It is not for the full, but for those who are conscious of need. It is not for the satisfied, but for those who yearn for the living bread that cometh down out of heaven. It is unto the hungry that the word cometh, "I will come in and sup with him and he with me."

TABLE DISMISSALS

1. "This is the bread which cometh down out of

heaven, that a man may eat thereof, and not die."
Enriched in the life of the soul, may you go in peace.

2. "Oh that men would praise the Lord for his goodness, and for his wonderful works to the children of men! For he satisfieth the longing soul, and the hungry soul he filleth with good."

3. Jesus taught us to pray, "Give us our daily bread;" at his table you have received the bread of life; in its strength, may you go in peace.

4. In one of the oldest Christian hymns we read, "The hungry he hath filled with good things; And the rich he hath sent empty away." May you who have been filled go in peace.

5. "Behold, the days come, saith the Lord God, that I will send a famine in the land, not a famine of bread, nor a thirst for water, but of hearing the words of the Lord." With that hunger appeased at the table of the Lord, may you go in peace.

6. We cannot partake of the bread of the Lord's Supper without thinking of those who lack sufficient physical bread. We pray here for forgiveness if our injustice has deprived anyone of life, that we may go in peace.

7. The ancient seer portrayed a time when men should hunger no more, neither thirst any more, for the Lamb would guide them unto the fountains of the waters of life. With this vision, go in peace.

JULY

We Have an Altar

"WE have a gymnasium;" such is the boast of a large number of churches. We have a recreational program for boys and girls, young people and adults. We teach them how to play, as well as how to pray. We give attention to the building up of the body, the temple of the Holy Spirit. We do not leave the recreation hours to the avarice of the commercial profiteer. Well do I remember my first position on leaving college, teaching in one of our mission high schools in China. I soon discovered that as much Christianity could be shared on the basketball floor as in the session of the Sunday-school class.

Other churches emphasize, "We have a kitchen." Our Ladies' Aid Society is famed over the countryside for its good suppers. In days of want, some churches have rendered a service in actually feeding the hungry, but in the main we have installed our kitchens in the church in order to promote fellowship. People never get so close together as when they put their feet under the same table while they break bread. When one dear old woman in my first parish objected to turning the house of God

[54]

into a cafeteria, I took real delight in pointing out to her that the meetings of the first Christians were for a common meal, filling the whole man.

Other churches would proclaim more æsthetic slogans. "We have an organ" is one that has a wide appeal. We have an instrument of exquisite tone, and an organist who knows how to arouse the deepest emotions! We have a choir trained to the peak of perfection, so that people come from all over the city to our special musical services! There can be no doubt that attractive music draws us; it seems to us an inseparable part of worship. I shall never forget the first time I heard the Saint Olaf choir sing its director's arrangement of "Fairest Lord Jesus." When they came to the great climax, a thrill of ecstasy went through me that left me limp.

There are churches which proudly boast, "We have a pulpit." The attention, of course, is not directed to the Italian carved oak, or the painted pine, whichever may adorn the platform, but to the eloquence of the voice that resounds from it. We have sermons that are clever and entertaining! We have messages that keep one abreast of modern affairs and familiar with the new books! We have a tradition of great preaching in this church. Well do I remember in my seminary days the thrill of expectancy with which I used to go down to Old South

Church, where George A. Gordon was lifting up
his mighty voice! How we would hang upon those
carefully chosen words and those closely knit ar-
guments!

I hope that I have said enough so that no one
imagines that I belittle any of these emphases, especially the last one. But I want to remind you
that in none of these things lies the distinctive con-
tribution of the church to our age. Every athletic
club provides a gymnasium, and most of our schools
have athletic facilities better supervised than we can
possibly provide. I have known some church basketball leagues which raised doubt about the Christian
value of much that goes on in our church gymnasi-
ums. Every lodge and society can at least engage
a kitchen for its social affairs. And some church
kitchens become in practice, not contributors to democratic social fellowship, but money-raising institutions
to take the place of direct giving. You can hear better music over the radio than all but a few churches
are able to provide. If we do go out and buy a
few hours' time of star soloists, we may only succeed
in turning the worship of God into a concert.

We shall never get enough good Christian preaching, but we should not forget that everyone has
preaching of a sort hurled at him from many di-
rections. Newspaper, magazine, stage, and forum

unite in what sometimes seems like the vain endeavor to lead the *thinking* of the masses. In none of these spheres is the church providing something unique.

There is one more slogan of which that cannot be said. "We have an altar!" We have a sanctuary dedicated to the worship of God. We have a symbol of his abiding and redeeming presence. We have an altar to which we may draw near with faith.

This is the slogan which motivates the modern emphasis upon worship. We have suddenly become conscious of our barren services and unpsychological orders of worship. We have looked around our churches and have discovered unsightly organ pipes and a prominent place for the minister directly in the center of attention. But where is the altar? Somewhat abashed, not a few churches have called in the architect to rearrange the interior fittings so that this article of furniture might be restored to its rightful place. I want to say in all earnestness, "No architect can put an altar in any church." Only a worshiping minister leading a worshiping congregation can erect an altar in the house of God.

As we read the pages of the Old Testament, we discover that men built altars wherever they were impelled to worship. It is not a crucifix which makes an altar; it is wherever men present their

sacrifices unto God. In many circles it is customary
to refer to the kneeling rail around the front of the
church as the altar. It is a fitting extension of ter-
minology if that is where we bring the spiritual sacrifice of ourselves, soul and body, and dedicate them
unto the Lord. Certainly, our altar is the communion table, for here is the visible expression of
our central act of worship.

I have taken this phrase from the Epistle to the
Hebrews. Throughout the entire letter it seems
that the author and his readers are suffering under
the palling contrast between the simple Christian
rites of worship and the elaborate ceremonies pre-
scribed for the Jewish tabernacle. It is not quite
clear whether he is referring to the Lord's Supper
when he triumphantly affirms, "We have an altar."
In any case, it was not a stone upon which victims
were slaughtered. The sacrifices with which God
was pleased were those of praise and thanksgiving.
The communion table does not become an altar for
us by associating with it the idea of the sacrifice of
a victim. It is our altar, because at this table we
find fellowship with God. It is our altar, because
as we kneel about it we bring the sacrifice of ourselves. It is our altar, because here we partake of
the symbols of the sacrifice of Him who has brought
God nearest unto men. We have an altar where, in

the breaking of bread, God's presence is manifest unto us.

TABLE DISMISSALS

1. You have knelt at the altar of praise and adoration, where with all the company of saints we laud and magnify His glorious name. Go in peace.

2. Paul found an altar to the unknown God. We kneel at the altar of Him, who is known to us through the cross of Christ. Go in peace.

3. As a live coal from off the altar purged the lips of the prophet of old, may we receive cleansing through these sacrificial elements. Go in peace.

4. May God so quicken the fire upon the altar of our hearts that the ashes of our burnt devotion may be fanned into a flaming heat. Go in peace.

5. We have an altar of forgiveness, a true mercy-seat. Leaving its protective covering, may you realize that it followeth with you. Go in peace.

6. An ancient seer pictured a bowl of incense on the altar in heaven, which were the prayers of the saints. We would bring such a sweet-smelling odor, the prayers of contrite hearts. Go in peace.

7. "To obey is better than sacrifice, and to hearken than the fat of rams." Our offering is not a material gift, but our loving obedience. Unto that service, go in peace.

The Silent Hour

SILENCE may indicate the poverty-stricken mind which knows nothing to say, or it may bespeak the composed receptiveness of alert faculties. Silence may result from the confused embarrassment of a muddled brain, or it may be the dramatic source of power of a master of audiences. There is the silence of the schoolboy who has forgotten his piece, and the silence of a George Arliss as he walks about the stage without uttering a syllable. There is the awkward pause when no one can think of a thing to say, and the silent hush of admiration for a speaker's eloquence.

Unembarrassed productive silence means that we have passed the portals of the superficial and entered into the deeper experiences of life. As Carlyle has said, "Silence is the element in which great things fashion themselves together. . . . Speech is of Time, Silence is of Eternity." There is a passive, dead silence, as well as the endless prattle in which small minds must always indulge, but Carlyle was thinking of the great experiences. There is the silence of the majestic forest; there is the silence of the endless sea; there is the silence of the rugged mountain peak; there is the silence of the arctic vastness.

But these are far removed from the everyday life of most of us. Instead, we are bombarded by a babel of sound from morning till night. When we retreat from the noise and confusion and retire to the quiet of our own fireside, we reach out into the invisible waves about us for voices that will save us from the dread calamity of stillness. Surely, in such a boisterous and talkative civilization as ours it is the peculiar mission of religion to cultivate the silent hour.

Silence ought not to be a Quaker idiosyncrasy for it marks many of the chief moments of religion. There is, first of all, the silence of waiting before God. The realization of the presence of God does not come to the person who is preoccupied with things. It comes to the person who actively prepares his mind for waiting on him. Saint John of the Cross, the Spanish mystic, once wrote, "The Eternal Father has spoken one word which is the Son, and he speaks it still in an Eternal Silence; the soul must listen to it in a like silence." Or, as the poet has reminded us,

> " 'Tis not in seeking,
> 'Tis not in endless striving

Thy quest is found;
Be still and listen,
Be still and drink the quiet
Of all around."

We do not call to a pagan deity who is deaf and must be awakened; we wait for the realization of the encompassing spiritual presence. It is not better ideas about God that will make him real to us. It is a period of expectant silence in which the way is made straight for his coming.

There is not only the silence of waiting upon God; there is the silence which comes to every humble spirit as he actually does face the determiner of destiny. The Hebrew prophet said, "The Lord is in his holy Temple; let all the earth keep silence before him." Again we read, "Hold thy peace at the presence of the Lord." Before the Lord of the universe, our idle words are little short of an impertinence. In democratic America we have little respect for the reverence demanded for the sovereign by court etiquette. We have sometimes rather foolishly talked about a democratic God. We are justified in rejecting the analogy drawn from absolute monarchs, but it is misleading to talk about a God for whom men would vote. A God who is the creature of men's choice is not a God at all. No analogy from modern democracies can illumine the

God whose overruling hand writes in the unfolding pages of history, and who speaks in the eternal silence of the soul. Before him we stand, and silence alone befits the awe which is inspired within us.

There is likewise another silence, the silence of communion. It is the culminating sacrament of every deep friendship. The silence of grief and the silence of death come knocking at our door; "we go forth to meet the silence of love." We seek that closer friend who will pierce beyond what words can utter to the deeper feelings that cannot be put into words. They radiate in the golden silence of perfect understanding. Communion may utilize language, but its rarest moments are in the silent hours where the hush is too holy to be interrupted by profane chatter.

If silence is the sacrament of human love, it is no less the medium of communion with God. "I have called you not servants but friends"—thus speaks the Eternal Word. We may share that friendship in whatever language is natural, but its holiest hours will call for silence. Unto that would Longfellow lead us when he wrote:

"Let us, then, labor for an inward stillness—
An inward stillness and an inward healing;
That perfect silence, where the lips and heart
Are still, and we no longer entertain

[63]

Our own imperfect thoughts and vain opinions,
But God alone speaks in us, and we wait
In singleness of heart, that we may know
His will, and in the silence of our spirits
That we may do his will, and do that only."

We are not met this morning to offer words in
tribute of silence. We are here to be "still and
know God." In silence we will wait for his coming
unto us; in silence we will bow before his presence;
in silence we will commune with him. Let no one
imagine that it will be easy to be still, even for a
few minutes, not knowing whether there is a choir
or a minister, not knowing who sits in the same pew,
not knowing the work of the week or the problems
that perplex us, only to be still and know God; to
know his gracious kindness and the beauty of his
holiness; to know the calm of his presence and the
joy of his friendship; to know, not because someone
is telling us things about which he has heard, but
because in the quiet stillness of the hour, God's
covenant is written in our hearts by the finger of
his Spirit.

In a few minutes we shall sing a hymn that we
all have sung many times before. We shall read
paragraphs and prayers that will present no novel
ideas, nor offer any new information. They are
words which will be but vain repetitions unless they

lead up to moments of luminous silence. These words of mine are simply reminders of what language cannot convey; they are but an invitation to join in this act of silence leading into the holy place of communion. There is only one voice that we are concerned to hear, "the still small voice of calm."

TABLE DISMISSALS

1. Let us meditate in silence upon the majesty of God. . . . Go in peace.

2. Let us meditate in silence upon the wisdom of God. . . . Go in peace.

3. Let us meditate in silence upon the loving-kindness of God. . . . Go in peace.

4. Let us meditate in silence upon his manifestation in the lives of all prophets, martyrs, and saints. . . . Go in peace.

5. Let us meditate in silence upon the Word which he has spoken unto men through Jesus. . . . Go in peace.

6. Let us meditate in silence upon the ideal which he has set before men. . . . Go in peace.

7. Let the words of our mouths and the meditations of our hearts be acceptable in thy sight, O Lord, our strength, and our redeemer. Go in peace.

The Offering of Labor

IN every communion service we read that Jesus took bread and blessed it. A divine blessing upon bread must include a blessing upon all of the labor that has been expended between the time the field was prepared for the sowing of wheat until the snowy loaf rests upon the table. The significance of such an act is plainer in contrast to the opening chapters of Genesis. When men gained their sustenance by the simple process of plucking fruit and nuts from the trees, human foresight and labor were unknown. We think of such primitive conditions as savagery. The ancient Hebrew writer looked upon them as the golden age. Labor was a curse heaped upon man by an offended Deity who said, "In the sweat of thy face shalt thou eat bread."

No one can deny that we enjoy bread only because some have toiled. When our grandmothers mixed and baked their own bread after rising at five in the morning, it was easier to remember the tilling of the soil, the gathering into barns, the grinding into flour, the baking, the distribution, and the manufacture of all of the implements used in that long process. Now when we step to the telephone and soon receive at our door a finished loaf in a sealed package, we are apt to forget that here is a symbol of the fact that life rests on human toil. Wheat may be a gift of God, but it is only by the sweat of man's brow that it is laid upon our table.

But does a curse rest upon labor? We have to confess that often it still does. A curse rests upon labor wherever the ideal of living without work is found. I do not refer, of course, to the young who look forward to their working days, or to the old who look back upon them. When some live in affluence and luxury because they "do not have to work," then is work a curse indeed. Their example brands work as a misfortune; and it needs must follow that if they live well without toiling, there must be others who toil without receiving the fruit of their labor. If such conditions have seemed remote from us in the past, they are no longer so. We have acquired our idle aristocracy; unemployment has placed hundreds of thousands on relief doles; rackets of every description have poisoned the minds of youths with the idea that since you can get money without working, labor is a curse to be avoided, not a necessity to be joyfully accepted.

Work is a curse wherever the drudgery of toil is excessive. That is inevitably a very vague phrase.

I am sure that there are some housewives who would insist upon including dish-washing in this oppressive drudgery. The stoker firing a furnace might insist that there could be no blessing upon his labor. We will not attempt to define the drudgery that is a curse, but pass immediately to the more important fact that the technician who invents useful machinery has been a leader in removing the curse from labor. Contrast the chains of Japanese women which I have seen at Nagasaki loading coal into the hold of a vessel, with the giant steam shovels that transfer five tons with one scoop as a single man operates a few buttons. Then you see what technology has done to lift the burdens from the backs of mankind. It has not all been gain. There is more curse in the monotonous tending of a repetitive machine than in creative hand labor; nevertheless, the machine has mediated great blessing to mankind.

But if the curse of work is really to be removed, the first cause must likewise be eliminated, the fact that men are so far from receiving the full fruit of their labor. Abraham Lincoln insisted that such was the rightful aim of government. We likewise insist that it is an imperative interest of religion. The religion which looks to a Nazarene carpenter as its leader is pledged to recover a blessing upon labor.

We would not minimize either of these endeavors; but while we wait for further inventions and while we work for a more just social order we must remember that it is within the spirit of man that the curse must ultimately be removed. L. P. Jacks has been one of the most eloquent preachers of the ethics of workmanship. He tells the story of a famous surgeon who was falsely supposed by some to be an atheist. His reply was, "If you want to know what my religion is, come and see me operate." Good work well done is the highest service we can render unto God and man. Jesus said, "The works that I do, . . . these bear witness of me." Work cannot be a curse if we see in it the greatest opportunity to show the sincerity and nobility of our life. It is a blessing where it is approached as a chance to reveal our faithfulness and accuracy, and the greatest skill we can acquire. True it is, "We earn our living by the quantity of work done; we save our souls by its quality."

In ancient Hebrew religion, the first fruits were brought as an offering unto God. When the early Christians worshiped in the breaking of bread, they first offered the bread and wine for which they had labored as a sacrifice unto God. I sometimes wish that we could renew that custom to-day. It is hardly a sufficient substitute to take an offering of alms for the poor. But if we do not each one of us bring bread as an offering to lay upon the altar, we may truly bring the offering of our labor. Labor Day is a recognition of the united efforts of workers on their own behalf. Labor Sunday is the most fitting time to dedicate our work as the expression of our service of God.

As we invoke a blessing upon this bread, we invoke a blessing upon all those whose sweat and blood and brain have brought it here. As we lift this bread unto God, it is a symbol of the whole social order which waits for the act of the Christian community in lifting it up unto God. Sacraments are not alone for the sanctuary. Unless they sanctify life, they remain a sterile thing apart. Unless this sacrament helps to redeem the curse from some bit of labor, it has been received in vain.

After Jesus had blessed the bread, he uttered the words, "This is my body." In other words, Christ is present in the world's work. The offering of the fruit of labor carries with it the offering of himself. He lives in the hearts of those who toil sincerely. He must find embodiment in all of the economic and industrial order that combines to put bread upon the tables of men and upon the table of the Lord. For the Lord of life has come down to live with those who work.

Table Dismissals

1. Jesus defended his ceaseless labor with the words, "My Father worketh hitherto." We worship a working God; with him may you work, that his peace may be yours.

2. There is no successful work without vision. May you rise from this table with new inspiration and zeal, refreshed for a task that has been illumined as you ate here with Christ, and may his peace be yours.

3. Jesus said, "Come unto me, all ye that labor and are heavy laden, and I will give you rest. Take my yoke upon you, . . . for my yoke is easy, and my burden is light." With such a companion in labor, go forth that peace may be yours.

4. "Behold, the hire of the laborers who mowed your fields, which is of you kept back by fraud, crieth out; and the cries of them that reaped have entered into the ears of the Lord of Sabaoth." May you rise and go forth to still those cries, that peace may be yours.

5. "Each man's work shall be made manifest; . . . and the fire itself shall prove each man's work of what sort it is." Unto the testing of life may you go to labor sincerely, that peace may be yours.

6. We cannot break bread with Christ without

sharing in the struggle that all may have enough to eat and to spare. Go forth to labor, that all may have food for the whole man, and peace will be yours.

7. We are told that God rested on the Sabbath day and hallowed it. A day of rest is hallowed by the days of toil which precede and follow. To sanctify this day of rest, may you return to offer your labor unto God, that his peace may be yours.

Lest We Forget

A HEBREW sage of long ago said, "Let him drink and forget his poverty, and remember his misery no more." Multitudes down the ages have followed his advice and have sought escape by one means or another from the storms that have made life too difficult. They have sought to drown their troubles in a sea of forgetfulness, and to escape to some world of illusion and dream.

Religion itself has sometimes appeared unto men as such an "escape." The Marxian slogan, "Religion is the opiate of the people," has a limited justification in some of its debased expressions. Religion has sometimes served as a sentimental salve to cover open sores which cried out for healing. It has occasionally offered men a comfortable ark where devotees might sing "Safe in the Arms of Jesus." It is true that religion calls for the smoking of the peace pipe, bringing true reconciliation unto men and cooling hatred and strife. It should never furnish an opium pipe, lulling men to sleep amid sin and wrong.

The religion which Jesus lived had no kinship to a soporific. He said, "I came to cast fire upon the earth; and what do I desire, if it is already kindled?" The Man who refused a narcotic drink which was offered to him as he was being nailed to the cross never sponsored a drink of forgetfulness. As Paul reports the communion cup, his words were, "This do as oft as ye drink it, in remembrance of me." The world may say, "Drink and forget;" Jesus said, "Drink and remember."

We have no right to forget the sacrifices of the past in our desire simply to enjoy the present. We enter into a heritage of mechanical invention, scientific discovery, literary creation, and political struggle that places us under a heavy debt of obligation. Our education is facilitated by centuries of culture. Every success we may attain is builded upon the achievements of those who have gone before. As the surface of a coral island lies on the dead bodies of billions of coral insects that have worked and died, so our lives rest on the struggles of those whom we have no right to forget. We could well adapt the words of Deuteronomy, "When the Lord thy God shall bring thee into the land; . . . great and goodly cities, which thou buildest not, and houses full of all good things, which thou filledst not, and . . . vineyards and olive trees, which thou plantedst not, . . . then beware lest thou forget."

We have no right to forget the needs of the

present. Poverty is not to be forgotten; it is to be removed. The industry of individuals will not suffice for that task; it is mockery for the successful man to say to the less fortunate, "Save and work, as I have done." Without a better organization of society we can never remove the curse of poverty. Misery is not to be forgotten but to be alleviated. The efforts of the unfortunate will not suffice without a society which remembers to provide hospitals for all and relief for the needy. Shall we forget the misery of crippled children and aged dependents, of the mentally deranged and the desperately discouraged? All of the best in man answers back that we have no right to forget the crying needs of the present which press in upon us unless in selfish isolation we shut our ears to those cries.

In a New Testament Epistle we read, "Remember Jesus Christ." Why should we remember him? It is not simply out of honor and respect. The hillsides of south China are covered with weather-beaten gravestones marking the mortal remains of centuries of yellow men. Wandering among them, you might imagine that no one remembered for whom those slabs had been erected. On the spring festival of Cing Ming, those hillsides are covered with family groups burning incense and token money in memory of the ancestors. It is a day dedicated to their honor and respect, "Lest we forget!" I do not think, however, that we are called upon to drink to the memory of Jesus lest he suffer personal oblivion.

We are not to remember for the purpose of revenge. The slogan that carried us into war with Spain was "Remember the Maine!" Why should we remember that one of our warships had been blown up in Cuban waters? In order to secure revenge. It is with shame that we recall the pogroms of Jews which have stained the pages of history of Christian countries. Men remembered Jesus Christ by taking revenge on the descendants of those who were reported to have called for his crucifixion. Nothing could be further from the spirit of One who said, "Love your enemies; pray for those who despitefully use you." It is said that the boy Hannibal was made by his father to swear undying hatred of Rome to right the wrongs of Carthage. But to remember Jesus Christ is not to perpetuate a feud, but to incarnate the only principle of reconciliation which life affords—that of love. We shall not forget that Jesus lived and died a Jew, and we welcome fellowship with those who bear that name.

Why, then, are we to remember Jesus Christ? The answer is as simple to state as it is difficult to perform. We would drink and remember in order to do his will. Often we sentimentally cherish the memento of a lost friend or loved one. But this memorial is more than a piece of sentimentality. If anyone sought the favor of Jesus by honeyed words of flattery, he always received a prompt rebuke. "Yea, rather, blessed are they that hear the word of God, and keep it." "Not everyone that saith unto me, Lord, Lord, shall enter into the kingdom of heaven; but he that doeth the will of my Father which is in heaven." We are to drink and remember Jesus Christ, in order to do his will.

"This do;" at first glance, that might appear to refer to eating and drinking together with him. It does link us closely to him, for there are few specific things that we could do as nearly as he did them on that last night. But we have missed the significance if we insist upon breaking a loaf, or quibble over the fermentation of the wine, or the mixing of it with water. We remember Jesus Christ, not as this act parallels an ancient meal, but as this act leads us deeper into his spirit. "This do;" those words must summon us to acts of kindness and deeds of generosity, to loving forbearance and costly devotion. "Lest we forget! Lest we forget!"

> "According to thy gracious word,
>   In meek humility,
> This will I do, my dying Lord,
>   I will remember thee."

TABLE DISMISSALS

1. As we drink of the cup of Christ, may we remember his devotion amid patience and tenderness toward men. In that spirit arise and go in peace.

2. We remember at this table the poverty of our own souls, and thirst to drink of a fountain of life. With satisfied hearts may you go in peace and the God of peace go with you.

3. We remember the toil of all who have gone before us, laboring to build the temple of society. To continue their sacrificial labors, go in peace.

4. While animals soon forget the past, it is the mark of a man to remember. As inheritors of the ages, go forth, and the peace of the eternal God go with you.

5. We remember God's provision in nature for our sustenance, our joy, and our comfort. With thankful hearts, go in peace.

6. We remember the high resolves of yesterday that have almost faded from our consciousness. May you go from this table to cherish with unforgetting zeal those unrealized dreams. Go in peace.

7. The dying thief said unto Jesus, "Remember me when thou comest in thy kingdom." May you go forth to remember him, that his kingdom may come for all. Go in peace.

[78]

The Heroic Temper

THERE is a myth which was widespread among both the Teutons and the Greeks of the conquest of a powerful dragon by a great hero. As the life blood oozed from the body of the dying dragon, a heavenly voice commanded the victor to bathe in the blood that he might become invulnerable. There was life-preserving power in the blood of the dragon. There is an old Christian hymn which has been beloved by generations of Christians:

> "There is a fountain filled with blood,
> Drawn from Immanuel's veins;
> And sinners plunged beneath that flood,
> Lose all their guilty stains."

There is sin-destroying power in the blood of the Lamb.

But these lines are not as popular with the present generation. Our sensibilities react against such a gory scene as a bath of blood. Removed from the emotional glow of a religious service, it appears to us both immoral and illogical that one could wash robes of character and make them white in the red blood of the Lamb. Nevertheless, our bloody theologies appear to be well-grounded in scripture. "Ye that were once far off are made nigh in the blood of Christ." The Epistle to the Hebrews fairly drips with blood, culminating in the dogmatic assertion, "No blood shed, no remission of sins."

This is all the more remarkable if we stop to consider that the crucifixion was accompanied by very slight loss of blood. The tradition is not unanimous that Christ was nailed to the cross instead of being tied. Assuredly, it was not the physical application of blood that any New-Testament writer had in mind. It has been suggested that "blood fellowship with Christ" is what is often meant. The ancient, primitive belief was that the life was in the blood. It was the blood of the sacrifice that was poured out on the altar. When the old sacrificial language was applied to the self-offering of Jesus for the cause of mankind, it was natural to speak of the blood of Christ. Redemption by the blood of Christ, then, means redemption by his sacrificial devotion, and our blood fellowship with that spirit.

The heroic temper is the indispensable price of worthwhile achievement. Truly has it been said: "If you succeed without suffering, it is because someone else has suffered without succeeding. If you suffer without succeeding, it is that someone after you may have an easier path." A frequent charge against the ethic of the New Testament is that it is ascetic and world-renouncing, while the spirit of the twentieth century is life-affirming. That is truer insight than much of our conventional morality that passes as Christian. But there is no appealing power in asceticism, nor any healing power in complacent, crowd morality. Neither is true to the mind of Jesus. He did not preach fasting, nor renunciation for the sake of renunciation. His ethic is heroic. His message is for heroes who are willing to do more than the average, who will throw all that they have and are into the one supreme cause.

The shedding of blood we connect at once with dying; it is very easy for us to sound the praises of Christian martyrs, for we live in an age of religious toleration. No one of us has the slightest chance of shedding a drop of blood in the name of Christ. We may shed real blood fighting for economic justice and racial fair play. That may truly be for his sake, but it is in living, not in dying, that our heroism will be demanded. Francis Asbury lived to ripe old age, but he knew what it was to have blood fellowship with Christ. Some complained of his power, but a biographer replies, "He had the power of riding six thousand miles a year at a salary of eighty dollars, through summer heat and winter cold, traveling in all weather and preaching in all places, his best covering from the rain often but a blanket, his best fare for six months in the twelve, coarse kindness, and his reward from too many, suspicion, envy, and murmurings all the year round."

Since those pioneer days civilization has tended to make us flabby and soft. We set a thermostat in a warm living room instead of getting up to stoke the fire on a zero morning. I do not propose that we should refuse modern inventions just for exercise in self-discipline. There are plenty of challenging causes to call for fortitude. The tragedy of our modern life is that the thermostat is symbolic of the amount of struggle and devotion and sacrifice that we are willing to make. Masses are incapable of heroic living; they are too self-centered for heroic giving; injustice and racketeering and suffering stalk abroad, because without the shedding of blood they cannot be removed.

We have made much of Jesus, the suffering victim, but not enough of Jesus, the sacrificing hero. We have too long thought of a helpless lamb, led dumb to the slaughter, which in some mysterious way would work for the salvation of men. We need to see the active hero, setting his face steadfastly toward Jerusalem, clearing the Temple of its unholy traffic, challenging the ruling interpretations of the law, and finally at the judgment bar appealing to the future for vindication; "Ye shall see the Son of man sitting on the right hand of power." The early Christians made much of the fact that the death of Christ was in fulfillment of prophecy. It does stand written in the Book of Life that there is no great conquest in a world estranged from God except through the shedding of blood.

The fourth Gospel reports a resurrection appearance to the disciples when Thomas was absent. He voiced his incredulity in the words, "I will not believe unless I can feel the print of the nails in his hands and in his feet." He spoke on behalf of a skeptical world. The power of the gospel lies in the cross, but men must always see the print of the nails. The Roman Catholic Church is right in requiring of all those for whom canonization is sought that they have brought one virtue to the heroic. Only heroic Christians can carry aloft the banner of Jesus Christ.

In Bernard Shaw's *Saint Joan*,[1] he portrays the social forces which led to the burning of the Maid of Orleans. In the epilogue, the main characters come back to life to give postmortem reflections. De Stogumber, a chaplain, prominent in the Inquisition trial, confesses: "I did a very cruel thing once

---

[1] Brentano's, New York. Reprinted by permission.

because I did not know what cruelty was like. I had
not seen it, you know. That is the great thing: you
must see it. And then you are redeemed and saved."

Cauchon, the presiding Bishop, asks, "Were not
the sufferings of our Lord Christ enough for you?"

"No. Oh, no; not at all. I had seen them in
pictures, and read of them in books, and been greatly
moved by them, as I thought. But it was no use:
it was not our Lord that redeemed me, but a young
woman whom I saw actually burnt to death."

The Bishop returned, "Must, then, a Christ perish in torment in every age to save those that have
no imagination?"

One must; we must. Men will not believe
unless they can see the nail-prints; they will not be
saved without the shedding of blood. On this table
are the emblems of sacrifice. We invite you to partake of them, that the heroic temper may be
strengthened in you.

Table Dismissals

1. One Christian hero wrote, "I rejoice in my
sufferings for your sake, and fill up on my part that
which is lacking of the afflictions of Christ in my
flesh." Unto the same ministry may you go, and
God's peace go with you.

2. Christ is to be found not at the end of a saw-

dust trail, but at the end of a blood-stained trail. In his fellowship may you go, who left his legacy of peace for you.

3. "Must Jesus bear the cross alone,
    And all the world go free?
No, there's a cross for everyone,
    And there's a cross for me."
Go in peace.

4. The cup has been called "a communion of the blood of Christ." Heroes have communion as they share a common passion. May you take from his table his passion and his peace.

5. We have wanted peace before any blood has been shed or any victory won. May you go from this table to finish the struggle that fuller peace may be yours.

6. If we walk in the light, as He is in the light, we have fellowship one with another, and the blood of Jesus his Son cleanseth us from all sin. Go in peace.

7. It is easy to drink wine at the communion table; it is not easy to "drink his blood." This wine becomes his blood as his sacrificial spirit is incarnate in us. Go in peace.

The Christian Mystery

IN the modern world mysteries connote popular murder stories; the readers are kept in suspense until the very end wondering who took the life of the victim. In the ancient world the mysteries were religious societies. They aimed to satisfy the suspense of men as to who could give them an immortal life. Through mysterious initiations and dramatic presentations the favored ones were to be assured a blessed life beyond.

It is pretty well established now that not a little of the language of the mysteries was appropriated by early Christians. Paul probably wrote to former members of the cult of Isis and those who had witnessed the Eleusinian mysteries. But when he spoke of a Christian mystery, it was not of something hidden. It was a message for all men. It was a mystery because its innermost nature was understood only by the one who had shared in the experience.

In First Timothy we read, "Great is the mystery of godliness." Men have traditionally been puzzled over the mystery of evil, and some have been led to believe that it makes faith in a good God impossible,

Waiving all presuppositions for the moment, suffering and evil present no problem at all. If we assume that life has emerged from a competitive struggle in an impersonal world, there is not the slightest reason to be surprised at the prevalence of the dark side of life. Under such conditions, the mystery is rather how godliness came to be. How did love and sacrifice, beauty and tenderness make their appearance?

It is a very specific aspect of the mystery of godliness of which the biblical writer spoke: "He who was manifested in the flesh, justified in the spirit, seen of angels, preached among the nations, believed on in the world, received up into glory." Christ was the mystery, and he remains an insoluble mystery if we exclude the Christian explanation. Any true interpretation of the universe must take into account his communion with the Father; the cause must at least equal the effect. There must be something to explain Jesus, and every other transcendent example of godliness. The mystery of godliness leads beyond that which the senses perceive, to an adequate solution of the mystery; to the Father.

We read of another mystery in the letter to the Colossians; it is "Christ in you." Those are words which puzzle the modern analytical student of personality. They belong to quite another world than "behavior patterns" and "fixations" and the rest of our psychological lingo. But the soberest scientist knows that after all of his experiments are made, inevitable mystery shrouds human personality; "It is a guest from the unseen." When the apostle affirmed, "I live; and yet no longer I, but Christ liveth in me," he was not offering an alternative to the latest psychological investigation. He was saying in his own way that "Your life is hid with Christ in God." He was appealing to an experience which united men with Christ so completely that he could either say "Christ in you" or "I in him."

"If any man is in Christ, he is a new creature." These are words which seem more easily understood. We are quite accustomed to similar claims. If any man be in Florida, or California, or the Riviera, he is a new creature. In a new environment under sunshiny skies we feel a new invigoration. But how can we be in Christ, if he is a man who lived nineteen hundred years ago? That is not a mystery but an impossibility unless "God was in Christ reconciling the world unto himself." We are in Christ and Christ in us when we are united with that spiritual presence who is known to us through Jesus as the Father.

The mystery of the indwelling Christ is, after all, the solution of the mystery of godliness. It is no longer vague and indefinite, but is clothed in the individuality of a person. We pray that the joy and friendliness which were in Christ may through his presence dwell in us; that the fearlessness and hot indignation against wrong which led him to drive the money-changers from the Temple may dwell in us; that the sincerity which despised all sham and the forgiving spirit which was in Christ on the cross may dwell in us. Truly could Paul say, "Christ in you, the hope of glory."

The Lord's Supper is not called a mystery in the New Testament, but early in the history of the church it became the Christian mystery *par excellence*. Protestants at once think of the doctrine of transubstantiation, of the belief that the bread and the wine are actually transformed so that their substance is no longer before us but is replaced by the substance of the body of Christ, the very same body that was born of the Virgin Mary. And we at once reply, "That is not a mystery but a magical superstition." But Protestants make a great mistake if they remove all of the element of mystery from this sacrament. We are not met simply to commemorate events which took place in ancient Palestine. We are met in the real presence of the Father of our Lord Jesus Christ.

Why should anyone hesitate to affirm that he is truly present? I do not mean that God is shut up

[89]

within a particle of food. The philosophers speak of the immanence of God; the humble Christian means the same thing when he says simply that God is near. God does not sit upon distant clouds watching the universe in impassive indifference; he is near: "Closer is He than breathing, and nearer than hands and feet." But the glib affirmation, "God is everywhere," cannot alter the fact that there is holy ground where his presence is peculiarly potent. Here is to be experienced that "diviner immanence" of which Bishop McConnell has written.

For the Christian there is a place of divinest immanence. It is the table of the Lord. It is where with the emblems of his sacrifice we re-enact the holy scene. In this act of sacred significance the Divine Presence is most surely to be found. Something material must always be the medium for the spiritual. For us, this table is the avenue of communion with him.

> "We taste thee, O thou Living Bread,
> And long to feast upon thee still;
> We drink of thee, the Fountain Head,
> And thirst our souls from thee to fill."

It is well known that the fourth Gospel contains no account of the institution of the Last Supper. The author has earlier presented Jesus as the bread of life upon whom believers shall feed. But he has not overlooked the permanent significance of the sacred meal. We read, "I am the vine, ye are the branches: He that abideth in me, and I in him, the same beareth much fruit." The wine is the fruit of the vineyard. Instead of saying, "Drink this in remembrance of me," the Christ of John affirms, "Abide in me." The drinking of the wine is the symbol of that abiding fellowship, so that we are in him, and he in us. We partake of these elements that something more than bread and wine may dwell in us; it is that "Christ may dwell in our hearts by faith"; for in the breaking of the bread he is truly present with us. That is the Christian mystery.

TABLE DISMISSALS

1. All life is a mystery. We cannot tell what distinguishes dead matter from a living cell with the power to grow. So is it with the life of the spirit. It is nourished by the mystery of mysteries. Go in peace.

2. Death is a mystery. Before it we are tempted to stand in fear. At the mystery of the Lord's Supper we learn that it is the road to life. Therefore, go in peace.

3. "Unto you it is given to know the mysteries of the kingdom of God." These words were spoken, not to the wise and the learned but to simple fisher-

men and peasants. Our mysteries are fathomed only by sincerity and love. Go in peace.

4. We are called to be "stewards of the mysteries." Ordinarily, men are asked to be guardians of the mysteries, but ours must be shared. To that ministry, go in peace.

5. The Ultimate must always be shrouded in mystery, but God has spoken to us in a Word which gives us the light we need. In that light may you go in peace.

6. It was a great mystery to the early Christians that in Christ the middle wall of partition between Jew and Gentile was broken down. May you go from this table to complete that mystery—the breaking down of all barriers that divide men.

7. Some have stumbled at the mystery of the real presence of Christ at his table. It is not a mystery to be solved, but a fact to be enjoyed. As you go, may the legacy of his peace go with you.

A Liturgy for Our Day

I OFFER here a liturgy in which the attempt is made to combine a sense of historical continuity with a recognition of the religious temper of our own time. The indebtedness to the liturgical treasures of the church will be obvious. Not a little has been derived from the Communion Service of Rudolph Otto, which has been included in his volume of *Religious Essays*. Valuable suggestions of Dr. Oscar Thomas Olson have been utilized. The service is not intended to replace any official liturgies, but to stimulate other ministers in adapting the communion to special groups and special needs.

The service opens, as is fitting in all worship, upon the note of praise. This is followed by the proclamation of the "Word of God" and the confession of man's sin. Opportunity is given for silent confession. It is my belief that this may be more personal than any liturgy can express. Most modern liturgies place the confession much later in the service. That is a survival from a division into two parts—a service of the Word, and the canon of the mass. The endeavor here has been to build a *unitary* service.

The communion message concludes the period of

instruction and confession, providing a transition to the announcement of divine grace. The presentation of the offering is retained at this point as a reminder that the communion elements were originally brought by the congregation. Though the emphasis upon personal sacrifice recurs later, this is the most fitting time for the visible demonstration of dedication.

Since the service of confession has preceded the message, the general invitation leads directly to the beautiful prayer of humble access, which has been freely adapted. As the *"Sursum corda"* goes back to the most primitive liturgies known, it is retained, though the dialogue had already become meaningless when the liturgy was divorced from a common meal.

The form of the prayer of consecration has been radically changed. The account of the Last Supper is not included as a pendent clause, but is taken out of the prayer, and the Gospel of Mark is quoted directly in an introductory "service of recollection." As it is seriously questioned by many historical scholars that Jesus deliberately intended to found a sacrament, no formula of "institution" is included. The actual prayer of consecration is short, and may be replaced by one directly related to the circumstances of the particular service.

The words of distribution are adapted from the

service of John L. Hunter. The beautiful forms from the *Book of Common Prayer* may be used by those who prefer them. The service ends upon the note of quiet gratitude for the divine grace, and of inward peace, which the world neither gives nor can take away.

The liturgy is printed with the sections in which the congregation is to join in capital letters. Indications of the order of service for a church calendar are printed in italics, as are also the brief words of instruction.

Communion Service

I. THE SERVICE OF PRAISE

The Organ Prelude
The Hymn of Praise
The Call to Worship

Let us worship the God who is Spirit.

GOD IS SPIRIT. THEY THAT WORSHIP HIM
MUST WORSHIP HIM IN SPIRIT AND IN
TRUTH.

Let us worship the God who is Light.

GOD IS LIGHT. IF WE WALK IN THE LIGHT
AS HE IS IN THE LIGHT, WE HAVE FEL-
LOWSHIP ONE WITH ANOTHER; AND
TRULY OUR FELLOWSHIP IS WITH THE
FATHER AND WITH HIS SON, JESUS
CHRIST.

Let us worship the God who is Power.

GOD IS POWER. THEY THAT WAIT UPON
THE LORD SHALL R E N E W THEIR
STRENGTH. THEY SHALL MOUNT UP
WITH WINGS AS EAGLES. THEY SHALL
RUN AND NOT BE WEARY. THEY SHALL
WALK AND NOT FAINT.

Let us worship the God who is Love.

GOD IS LOVE. EVERYONE THAT LOVETH IS BORN OF GOD AND KNOWETH GOD; AND WE KNOW THAT WE HAVE PASSED FROM DEATH UNTO LIFE BECAUSE WE LOVE.

The Gloria Patri

GLORY BE TO THE FATHER, AND TO THE SON, AND TO THE HOLY GHOST; AS IT WAS IN THE BEGINNING, IS NOW AND EVER SHALL BE, WORLD WITHOUT END. AMEN.

The Collect for Purity

ALMIGHTY GOD, UNTO WHOM ALL HEARTS ARE OPEN, ALL DESIRES KNOWN, AND FROM WHOM NO SECRETS ARE HID, CLEANSE T H E THOUGHTS OF OUR HEARTS BY THE INSPIRATION OF THY HOLY SPIRIT, THAT WE MAY PERFECTLY LOVE THEE, AND WORTHILY MAGNIFY THY HOLY NAME, THROUGH JESUS CHRIST OUR LORD. AMEN.

The Lord's Prayer

OUR FATHER, WHO ART IN HEAVEN: HAL-LOWED BE THY NAME, THY KINGDOM COME, THY WILL BE DONE, ON EARTH AS

IT IS IN HEAVEN. GIVE US THIS DAY OUR
DAILY BREAD. AND FORGIVE US OUR
TRESPASSES, AS WE FORGIVE THOSE WHO
TRESPASS AGAINST US. AND LEAD US NOT
INTO TEMPTATION, BUT DELIVER US
FROM EVIL. FOR THINE IS THE KING-
DOM, AND THE POWER, AND THE GLORY,
FOR EVER. AMEN.

II. THE SERVICE OF INSTRUCTION AND CONFES-
SION

*The Reading of the Scriptures (lesson for
the day)*

The Ideal of the Gospel

Hear the teaching of the gospel: Thou
shalt love the Lord thy God with all thy
heart, and with all thy soul, and with all
thy strength, and with all thy mind: and
thy neighbor as thyself.

No man can serve two masters. Ye cannot serve God and Mammon. Lay not up
for yourselves treasures upon the earth,
but lay up for yourselves treasure in
heaven, for where thy treasure is, there
will thy heart be also.

If ye forgive men their trespasses, your
heavenly Father will also forgive you.

[98]

But if ye forgive not men their trespasses, neither will your Father forgive your trespasses.

Love your enemies, and pray for them that persecute you, that ye may be sons of your Father.

Whosoever would become great among you, shall be your minister; and whosoever would be first among you shall be servant of all.

The Service of Confession

Let us examine ourselves in the presence of the Eternal, who searcheth the hearts of men, for he would not have us come to the table of the Lord in an unworthy manner.

WE CONFESS THAT WE HAVE SINNED IN THOUGHT, WORD AND DEED.

(*Period of silence*)

Almighty God, our Heavenly Father, who of thy great mercy hast promised forgiveness of sins to all them that with hearty repentance and true faith turn unto thee, have mercy upon us; pardon and deliver us from all our sins; confirm and strengthen us in all goodness; and bring us to everlasting life, through Jesus Christ, our Lord. AMEN.

The Pastoral Prayer
The Agnus Dei (or a choral response or devotional anthem)
The Communion Message

III. THE OFFERING AND SACRIFICE

Worship in the presentation of offerings (The minister will introduce with appropriate passages and at the presentation of the gifts the congregation will sing:)

ALL THINGS COME OF THEE, O LORD, AND OF THINE OWN HAVE WE GIVEN THEE.

(At this time, if it is desired, members may be received into the church as an expression of their sacrificial dedication of life.)

IV. THE CONSECRATION OF THE ELEMENTS

(After the uncovering of the table, the minister will say:)

The General Invitation

Ye that do truly and earnestly repent of your sins, and are in love and charity with your neighbors, and intend to lead a new

[100]

life following the commandments of God, and walking from henceforth in his holy ways, draw near with faith, and take this holy sacrament to your comfort. Let us pray:

The Prayer of humble access

We do not presume to come to this thy table, O merciful Lord, trusting in our own righteousness, but in thy manifold and great mercies. We are not worthy so much as to gather up the crumbs under thy table. But thou art the same Lord, whose property is always to have mercy. Grant us, therefore, so to partake of these emblems of the passion of thy Son, that we may evermore dwell in him, and he in us. AMEN.

The Sursum Corda

Lift up your hearts.

WE LIFT THEM UP UNTO THE LORD.

Let us give thanks unto the Lord.

IT IS MEET AND RIGHT TO DO SO.

The Preface and Sanctus

It is very meet, right, and our bounden duty that we should at all times and in all

places give thanks unto thee, O Lord,
Holy Father, Almighty, Everlasting
God.

THEREFORE WITH ANGELS AND ARCHAN-
GELS, AND WITH ALL THE COMPANY OF
HEAVEN, WE LAUD AND MAGNIFY THY
GLORIOUS NAME, EVERMORE PRAISING
THEE, AND SAYING: HOLY, HOLY, HOLY,
LORD GOD OF HOSTS, HEAVEN AND
EARTH ARE FULL OF THY GLORY.
GLORY BE TO THEE, O LORD, MOST
HIGH! AMEN.

The Service of Recollection

Hear the words of the gospel according
to Mark: And as they were eating, he
took bread, and when he had blessed, he
brake it, and gave to them, and said, Take
ye: this is my body. And he took a cup,
and when he had given thanks, he gave
to them: and they all drank of it. And
he said unto them, This is my blood of
the covenant, which is poured out for
many. Verily, I say unto you, I shall no
more drink of the fruit of the vine, until
that day when I drink it new in the kingdom of God.

The Prayer of Consecration

And now, in his name, we take these gifts of bread and wine to be set apart by the Holy Spirit in prayer and thanksgiving.

Father of all mercies and God of all comfort, we humbly beseech thee to grant us thy presence and so sanctify these creatures both of bread and wine, that we may receive by faith Christ crucified in us, and that he may be one with us and we with him. AMEN.

O Lord, our Heavenly Father, we thy humble servants desire thy Fatherly goodness mercifully to accept this our sacrifice of praise and thanksgiving. And here we offer and present unto thee, O Lord, ourselves, our souls and bodies, to be a reasonable, holy, and living sacrifice unto thee; humbly beseeching thee that all we who are partakers of this holy communion may receive thy grace and heavenly benediction, through Jesus Christ, our Lord. AMEN.

V. THE COMMUNION

The Distribution of the bread

Let us eat of this bread in remembrance of

Christ; and may the life which was in him
be in us also.

The Distribution of the cup

Let us drink of this cup in remembrance
of Christ; and may the spirit in which he
died be in us also.

*(If communion be at the altar rail, the
tables may be dismissed with appropriate
words of Scripture or sentences related to
the message of the day; a verse of a hymn
should be sung as the people come to the
table. If communion be received in the
pews, a verse of a hymn may be sung as
the deacons return to the front of the
church.)*

VI. The Post-Communion

Lord, now lettest thou thy servant depart
in peace, according to thy word.

FOR MINE EYES HAVE SEEN THY SALVA-
TION.

Praise the Lord, O my soul, and all that
is within me praise his holy name.

PRAISE THE LORD, O MY SOUL, AND FOR-
GET NOT ALL HIS BENEFITS.

[104]

The Lord be with you.

AND WITH THY SPIRIT.

The peace of God, which passeth all understanding, keep your hearts and minds in the knowledge and love of God, and of his Son, Jesus Christ our Lord; and the blessing of God Almighty, the Father, the Son, and the Holy Spirit, be among you and remain with you always.